◆ HISTORY FROM PHOTOGRAPHS ◆

Journeys

Kath Cox and Pat Hughes

Wayland

Notes for Parents and Teachers

This book provides a flexible teaching resource for Early Years history. Two levels of text are given – a simple version and a more advanced and extended level. The book can be used for:

- ◆ Early stage readers at Key Stage 1
- ◆ Older readers needing differentiated text
- ◆ Non-readers who can use the photographs
- ◆ Extending skills of reading non-fiction
- ◆ Adults reading aloud to provide a model for non-fiction reading

By comparing photographs from the past and the present, children develop skills of observation, ask questions and discuss ideas. They should begin by identifying the familiar in the modern photographs before moving on to the photographs from the past. The aim is to encourage children to make 'now' and 'then' comparisons.

The use of old photographs not only provides an exciting primary resource for history but, used alongside the modern photographs, aids the discussion of the development of photography. Modern photographs in black and white are included to encourage children to look more closely at the photographs and avoid seeing the past as 'black and white'. All the historical photographs were taken beyond the living memory of children and most have been selected from the Edwardian period between 1900–20. A comprehensive information section for teachers and other adults on pages 29–31 gives details of each of the old photographs, where known, and suggests key points to explore and questions to ask children.

Editor: Vanessa Cummins
Designer: Michael Leaman
Photostylist: Zöe Hargreaves
Production Controller: Nancy Pitcher
Consultants: Suzanne Wenman and Peter Chrisp

Front cover: The main photograph is of a paddle-steamer in Fleetwood, Lancashire, taken by Francis Firth & Co in 1908. The inset photograph is of a P&O ferry, the *Pride of Le Havre*.
Endpapers: Photographers at work at a wedding, 1907.
Title page: Mr J. Inch and bicycle, Exeter, 1901.

Picture Acknowledgements:
The publishers would like to thank the following for the use of their photographs: Bolton Metro Museum 9; Defence Research Agency, Farnborough 21; Mary Evans Picture Library 7, 11, 15, 23; Francis Firth & Co **main cover picture**, 25; Hulton Deutsch 13, 19; The Department of Engineering, Liverpool University 27; P&O Ferries **inset cover picture**; Royal Photographic Society, Bath, endpapers, contents page; Topham 5, 17. All other pictures are from the Wayland Picture Library. All artwork is by Barbara Loftus.

First published in 1995 by Wayland (Publishers) Limited
61 Western Road, Hove, East Sussex BN3 1JD, England

© Copyright 1995 Wayland (Publishers) Limited

The right of Kath Cox and Pat Hughes to be identified as the authors of this work has been asserted in accordance with the Copyright, Designs and Patents Act 1988.

British Library Cataloguing in Publication Data
Cox, Kath
Journeys. – (History from Photographs Series)
I. Title II. Hughes, Pat III. Series
388.09
ISBN 0-7502-1538-0 HARDBACK
ISBN 0-7502-2121-6 PAPERBACK

Typeset in Britain by Michael Leaman Design Partnership
Printed and bound in Italy by G. Canale & C. S.p.A.

·Contents·

A Brownie box camera and case, 1900.

Some of the more difficult words appear in **bold** in the text
and are explained in the picture glossary on page 28.
The pictures will help you to understand the entries more easily.

Ahmed and his mum walk to school.

Ahmed lives near his school so he walks there and back. He walks along a road which is busy with fast cars. His mum walks with him. If it rains they go in a car.

4

Most children walked to school on their own.

Some children had to walk a long way to school. The roads were quiet with few cars. Some children walked with their older brothers and sisters. When school finished, they had to walk home again.

Emma and Paul like riding their bicycles.

The bicycles have light **frames** and comfortable **saddles**.
Cyclists wear helmets and knee pads to protect them if they fall off.

Many people liked to go for bicycle rides for fun.

Some people travelled to work on bicycles.
Bicycles had heavy frames and hard saddles.
People rode their bicycles wearing everyday clothes.

This car is parked
outside the home
of the Jones family.

Many people own cars today.

Cars can go very fast on good roads.

Cars are warm and comfortable to ride in.

This family are going for a drive in their car.

Few people owned cars.
Cars had just been invented and were very slow.
They were cold and bumpy to ride in.

This is a double-decker bus.

It can carry lots of **passengers**.
The bus has an engine which makes the bus move.
Passengers buy a bus ticket from the driver.

This bus was pulled by horses.

Passengers on the top deck got wet and cold in bad weather.
They paid half price if they sat upstairs.
A **bus conductor** took their money and gave them a ticket.

This is a taxi cab.

Taxis are warm and comfortable to travel in.
Passengers talk to the taxi driver through a window
between the front and back seats.
A meter shows the passengers how much to pay.

This is a hansom cab.

The seats in hansom cabs were padded because the roads were often bumpy. Passengers spoke to the driver through a hole in the roof. The driver charged a fare at the end of the journey.

This town is busy.

The pavements are crowded with people walking.
There are different kinds of **vehicles** on the road.
The street is noisy with the sound of cars.

This town was very busy too.

There were crowds of people walking along the street.
Horse-drawn **trams**, buses and hansom cabs waited for passengers.
Drivers shouting at their horses made this street noisy.

This is a diesel train.

Diesel trains can travel long distances very quickly.
They are powered by diesel engines.
The driver is warm and comfortable inside the train.

This is a steam train.

People travelled by steam train on long journeys.
Trains were the fastest way to travel 100 years ago.
Steam engines were powered by burning coal.
The driver got very dirty because of the smoke.

This is Waterloo Station in London.

The station is busy with passengers waiting for a train to France.
They are looking up at a board to see what time the train will leave.
The passengers carry their own **luggage** to the train.

Waterloo station is busy with people going on holiday.

People travelled by train to the seaside.

Passengers showed their ticket to the guard and then got on to the train.

Porters carried luggage on **trolleys** and put it on the train.

This aeroplane is getting ready to take off.

Aeroplanes take off from **runways**.

Aeroplanes are the fastest way to travel.

Jumbo jets like this carry over 300 passengers and **crew**.

Travelling by aeroplane is warm and comfortable.

This was one of the first aeroplanes to be made.

Aeroplanes took off from grassy fields.
Aeroplanes could not fly very far or fast.
There was only enough room for the **pilot**.
He or she would get cold and wet on the journey.

The driver sits at the front to drive the tram.

Trams run on rails in the road.

The tram only has one deck.

It is powered by electricity from a wire above the road.

Only a few cities have trams today.

This driver stands at the front to drive the tram.

The tram has two decks. The top deck is open.
People are watching because it is
the first time this tram made a journey.
Most cities had trams in 1905.

This car ferry is sailing into port.

Car ferries are very large.
They carry cars, lorries, **cargo containers** and passengers
on short journeys across the sea.

This is a paddle-steamer.

Paddle-steamers carried passengers and cargo.
The steam engines turned the paddle-wheels and pushed
the boat through the water.

This is the port of Dover.

Dover is a busy port.

Cargo containers are driven on to ships to be taken to Europe.

People come to Dover to go on holiday.

Foot passengers walk on to the ferry. Cars and vans are driven on.

This is the port of Liverpool nearly eighty years ago.

The port was busy with goods being loaded on to ships. Goods were sent to the USA, Australia and Canada. Passengers who wanted to live in other countries also sailed from Liverpool.

· Picture Glossary ·

 **bus conductor** A person who sells tickets on a bus.

 **pilot** A person who flies an aeroplane.

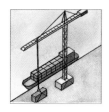 **cargo containers** Large, metal boxes which are used to move things from one place to another by ship, aeroplane or lorry.

 **runways** Flat areas made for aeroplanes to land on and take off from.

 **crew** People who work on aeroplanes.

 **saddles** The padded seats on bicycles.

 **frames** The main part of bicycles, made from metal.

 **trams** Buses that run on rails in the road and are powered by electricity.

 **luggage** Bags and cases that people carry when they are travelling.

 **trolleys** Small vehicles with wheels used for moving things.

 **passengers** People who make a journey on a bus or other kind of transport.

 **vehicles** Forms of transport, usually with wheels and used on roads.

· Books to Read ·

Bikes by Trevor Lord (Amazing series, Dorling Kindersley, 1992).
Cars by G. Tanner and T. Wood (History Mysteries series, A & C Black, 1992).
Cars by R. Thomson (Changing Times series, Franklin Watts, 1991).
Flying Machines by Robin Kerrod (Amazing series, Dorling Kindersley, 1992).
How We Travelled by S. Ross (Starting History series, Wayland, 1991).
Incredible Flying Machines (Snapshot series, Dorling Kindersley, 1994).
Transport by Nigel Flynn (Looking Back series, Wayland, 1991).
Travel and Transport by H. Edom (Living Long Ago series, Usborne, 1990).

· Places to Visit ·

Many local museums have small collections of vehicles, so it is worth contacting them to see what they can offer. The following examples are specialist museums.

The Boat Museum Trust
Dockyard Road
Ellesmere Port
South Wirral L65 4EF

    Tel: 0151 355 5017
    Education Officer: Annette Cavell

London Transport Museum
Covent Garden
London WC2E 7BB

    Tel: 0171 379 6344
    Education Officer: Stephen Allen

The Welsh Industrial
and Maritime Museum
Bute Street, Pierhead
Cardiff CF2 6AN

    Telephone: 01222 481919
    Education Officer: Rhian Thomas

The Birmingham Museum
of Science and Industry
Newhall Street
Birmingham B3 1RZ

    Telephone: 0121 235 3890

The Glasgow Museum of Transport
Kelvin Hall
1 Bunhouse Road
Glasgow G3 8PD

    Telephone: 0141 221 9600

The Ulster Folk and Transport Museum
153 Bangor Road
Holywood
Belfast BT18 OEU

    Telephone: 0232 428428
    Education Officer: Deirdre Brown

· Further Information about the Photographs ·

PHOTOGRAPH ON PAGE 5
School children, Leamington Whitmarsh, Warks, 1892.

About this photograph
Walking was the most common way of getting around. The first practical car was invented in the 1880s, but it was not until 1909 that Ford produced his famous 'Model T'. Horse-drawn buses and electric trams were common forms of transport, but only in urban areas.

Questions to ask
What kind of shoes are the children wearing?
Did people get more exercise walking than people do today?

Points to explore
People – activities, number, clothes.
Background – buildings, street furniture, the pavement.

PHOTOGRAPH ON PAGE 7
A group of cyclists c.1900.

About this photograph
Cycling appealed to all classes, rich and poor. Cycling was both a means of transport and a popular pastime. The invention of air-filled, pneumatic tyres in 1888 made bicycles much more comfortable and lighter. Cyclists wore knee breeches, caps and short jackets as cycling wear. Some women cyclists wore knickerbockers, but this was considered very shocking.

Questions to ask
How did the cyclists warn people to get out of their way?
Did the cyclists know the photograph was being taken? How can you tell?

Points to explore
Bicycles – different parts, accessories, materials, range of models.
People – ages, clothing, pose.

PHOTOGRAPH ON PAGE 9
A family outing in an early car, Bolton, 1905.

About this photograph
The car was made by the Vulcan Motor Company in Southport, Lancashire, and was owned by the manager of a local colliery. Few people had cars as they were expensive to manufacture. In 1900, there were only 8,500 cars in Britain. The top speed of the car was 65 kmh. Today, a modern car, such as the Citroen ZX, has a top speed of 165 kmh.

Questions to ask
Who are the people in the photograph?
Where might they have been going?
How are the passengers protected from the cold?

Points to explore
The cars – tyres, lights, steering wheel, horn, design, speed.
The passengers – clothing, comfort, reasons for travelling.

PHOTOGRAPH ON PAGE 11
A horse-drawn bus in London c.1900.

About this photograph
Most buses were horse drawn until the early 1900s when the petrol engine was introduced. The horses had to be changed regularly because it was such hard work. The horses wore blinkers to stop them being frightened or distracted by the vehicles around them.

Questions to ask
Where is the bus going?
Who can you see on the bus?
How did the driver steer the horses?

Points to explore
Vehicles – clothing, activity.
Background – buildings, road surface, advertising.

PHOTOGRAPH ON PAGE 13
A hansom cab, London, 1905.

About this photograph
In 1905, hansom cabs were the equivalent of the modern taxi. The driver stood on the back of the cab with the reins across the roof. He communicated with the passengers through a small lid in the roof of the cab. Hansom cabs had solid wheels which made the journey bumpy for the passengers.

Questions to ask
Did the driver have a good view of the road? Why?
How would a passenger get into the hansom cab?
Would the passenger be comfortable? Why?

Points to explore
Vehicles – shape, size, wheels, lights, method of steering.
People – clothing, activities.

PHOTOGRAPH ON PAGE 15
Street scene in Piccadilly Square, Manchester c.1890

About this photograph
The photograph gives an idea of how busy the centre of a Victorian town could be. A variety of methods of travelling can be seen – walking, hansom cabs, horse-drawn buses and trams. The street would have been quieter and less polluted than a street today, although horse dung on the road must have been a common sight!

Questions to ask
What different ways of travelling can you see?
What sounds would you hear?

Points to explore
Vehicles – names, power, size, loads.
Background – buildings, street furniture, road surfaces.
People – gender, ages, clothes, activities, occupations.

Steam train on the Great Western Railway, c.1900.

About the photograph
The railway provided the fastest way to travel from the 1890s to the 1950s. At first, there were three classes of travel, First, Second and Third. Steam engines were not a clean form of transport. If a passenger looked out of the train while it was moving he or she got covered with black 'smuts' (soot).

Questions to ask
What is the train's name and number?
Who is with the driver? What was his job?

Points to explore
Engines – size, shape, wheels, lights.
Carriages – number, design, windows, doors.

Waterloo railway station, London, 1912.

About this photograph
The railway provided the fastest and most efficient form of long-distance travel. Stations had high roofs to allow steam and smoke from the engines to escape. Waterloo has recently had a terminal built for the high speed link between London and Paris via the Channel Tunnel.

Questions to ask
How do the people know which train to get on?
Where are the trains positioned on the modern photograph?

Points to explore
Trains – engines, carriages.
Background – structure, roof, lighting, signs, advertising.
People – station workers, passengers, clothing, luggage.

A Cody monoplane, Farnborough, Surrey, 1910.

About this photograph
Air transport was in its infancy in the 1900s, but it grew very quickly. The first powered flight ever recorded was by Orville Wright, in the USA, in 1903. The early aeroplanes were flimsy structures which offered little protection to the pilot. By 1935, there were nineteen airlines in Britain, with seventy-six services, carrying 121,559 passengers.

Questions to ask
Where would the pilot sit?
Would the aeroplane be uncomfortable? Why?
Would the aeroplane be safe? Why?

Points to explore
Aeroplanes – design, structure, materials, wheels, wings.
Background – buildings, people, runway.

The Finsbury Park – Enfield Tram Service, 1905.

About this photograph
Electric trams were competing with horse-drawn trams by 1900. Passengers had to be aware of other vehicles when boarding because they had to get on and off in the middle of the road (trams could not pull into the kerb). At some road junctions there was a delay because the conductor had to stop the tram to lift the electric arms from one set of overhead wires to another.

Questions to ask
How did the driver see at night or when it was foggy?
What kind of people were the passengers?

Points to explore
Background – the kind of street, the crowd, date of buildings.
Tram – size, method of steering, advertising, power.

A paddle-steamer, Fleetwood, 1908.

About this photograph
Paddle-steamers were a familiar sight in the early 1900s as they carried passengers and goods around the coast and along rivers. Two paddle-wheels pushed the boat along. The wheels were powered by steam. This form of power was gradually replaced by diesel and petrol-driven engines.

Questions to ask
What different kinds of boat can be seen?
Which boat would move the fastest?
What do you think the children are doing?

Points to explore
Boats – different sizes, shapes, design, power sources.
People – ages, clothes, activities.

The port of Liverpool c.1919.

About this photograph
Liverpool was a thriving port at this time. There was the normal river traffic across the Mersey, bringing people to work and shop in the city. Also, thousands of families emigrating to the USA, Canada and Australia in search of a better life left from the port of Liverpool. Ships transported goods to Liverpool from all over the world, particularly to and from countries in the British Empire.

Questions to ask
What are the people doing?
Where might they be going?

Points to explore
Ships/boats – size, shape, design, power source.
Background – buildings, machinery and equipment.
People – appearance, clothes.

· Index ·

(Items that appear in the text)